CURIOUS

ABOUT THE

WHITE HOUSE

by Kate Waters

GROSSET & DUNLAP

An Imprint of Penguin Random House

GROSSET & DUNLAP

Penguin Young Readers Group
An Imprint of Penguin Random House LLC

This trademark is owned by the Smithsonian Institution and
is registered in the U.S. Patent and Trademark Office.

Smithsonian Enterprises:
Christopher Liedel, President
Carol LeBlanc, Senior Vice President, Education and Consumer Products
Brigid Ferraro, Vice President, Education and Consumer Products
Ellen Nanney, Licensing Manager
Kealy Gordon, Product Development Manager

Smithsonian Institution, National Portrait Gallery:
James G. Barber, Historian

PHOTO CREDITS: **JFK LIBRARY:** 21 (bottom, right). **LIBRARY OF CONGRESS:** 1, 4, 5, 6, 7, 9, 12, 13 (bottom), 14–15, 17 (top),
28 (top), 32. **NATIONAL ARCHIVES:** 17 (bottom), 20, 21, 22 (bottom), 23, 24 (bottom), 25, 27, 28 (left, bottom right), 29 (bottom).
SMITHSONIAN NATIONAL MUSEUM OF AMERICAN HISTORY: 11, 13 (top), 26. **SMITHSONIAN NATIONAL PORTRAIT GALLERY:** 8, 10.
THINKSTOCK: front cover (photo by toddtaulman), back cover (photo by mj00007), 3 (photo by pantone 6), 4 (photo by ke77kz),
18–19 (photo by tomwachs), 30–31 (photo by Sean Pavone). **WHITEHOUSE.GOV:** 16, 22 (top), 24 (top), 29 (top).

What's the most famous address in the United States? 1600 Pennsylvania Avenue,

WELCOME TO THE WHITE HOUSE

PL   ON

the White House!

It has been home to US presidents, first ladies, first children, even first pets for more than 200 years.

Come on into this famous building.

The White House is in Washington, DC, the capital of the United States. In 1790, George Washington, the first US president, and Congress decided that the new country needed a new capital city. It should include a president's house and a building where Congress could meet.

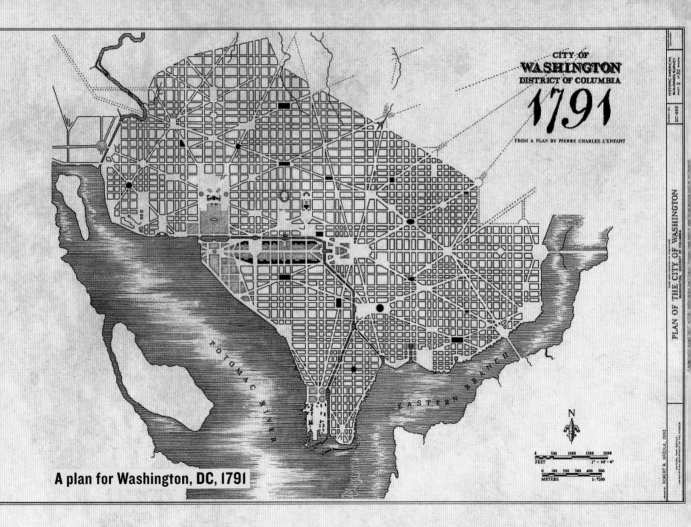

A plan for Washington, DC, 1791

The White House in the twentieth century

Washington chose a patch of farmland where the Potomac River flows between Maryland and Virginia. At the time, the United States was very small. This area was at its center. Washington had plans drawn up for a new city. He held a contest to design the president's house. James Hoban, an Irish-born architect, won.

WASHINGTON

New York. Published by M. Morris at the Shield Sep.r 1st 1795, & as according to Act of Parliament by G. I. Parkyns, Esq.r London.

Near the Potomac River in 1795

At the time, Washington, DC, was a swamp! Thousands of mosquitoes buzzed around the hot, muddy place where the White House would be built. Workers had to drain water from the lowland before they could clear it. It took almost eight years to build the White House. By then, George Washington had retired, and John Adams was president.

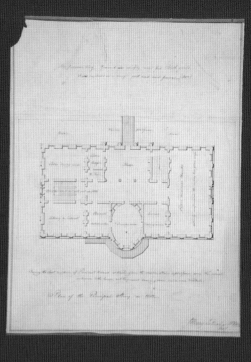

Floor plans from 1803 to 1807

The building was first called the President's House or the Executive Mansion.

John Adams and his wife, Abigail, moved into the President's House in 1800. It wasn't very presidential! It wasn't even fully built!

John Adams was president from 1797 to 1801.

Abigail kept fires lit in every fireplace because the rooms were damp. She hung freshly washed clothes to dry in the unfinished East Room instead of outside where people could see them.

First Lady Abigail Adams

In 1812, the United States went to war with Britain. Some battles took place near Washington, DC. British soldiers burned the city and set fire to the President's House in 1814. First Lady Dolley Madison is famous for saving a picture of George Washington. It hangs in the White House today.

A copy of this painting was saved.

After the fire, the building was painted white to cover the smoke stains. People began to call it the White House. President Theodore Roosevelt made the name official

The White House changed over time. Two covered main entrances, the North Portico and the South Portico, were built in the 1800s. It became more comfortable when plumbing, gas lighting, and central heating were added between 1833 and 1853.

President Theodore Roosevelt had the West Wing built in 1902. He had six children and needed a quiet place to work and receive visitors.

Eventually, the Oval Office was built in the West Wing. It is still where the president works.

The Roosevelts, 1903. Theodore Roosevelt was president from 1901 to 1909.

President Woodrow Wilson's sheep, in front of the South Portico. Wilson was president from 1913 to 1921.

The White House has
six floors and is used
in four important ways.

West Wing

It is an office.

It is the nation's welcoming stage.

East Wing

It is a home.

It is a museum.

President Barack Obama was elected in 2008 and again in 2012.

Hundreds of people are in the White House every day. The president, vice president, first lady, staff, and press all have offices there.

The president's main office is in the West Wing. It's called the Oval Office because of its shape. There are two flags behind the president's desk. One is the flag of the United States. The other is the presidential flag. The vice president also has an office in the West Wing.

The presidential seal is molded in plaster

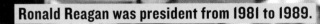

Ronald Reagan was president from 1981 to 1989.

Franklin Delano Roosevelt and friends in the Oval Office with his birthday cake. He was president from 1933 to 1945.

Reporters have offices near the president so they can keep up with the president's news.

The first lady and her staff work in offices on the second floor of the East Wing. On the South Lawn, outside the West Wing, there is a landing area for the president's helicopter, Marine One.

A cool way to get to and from the White House!

Rolling out the rug for guests in the Diplomatic Reception Room

First Lady Laura Bush in the State Dining Room. Her husband, George W. Bush, was president from 2001 to 2009.

The president greets and entertains people on the ground floor of the White House. Visitors usually enter under the North Portico. Sometimes the president's band plays.

These rooms may also be used when guests come to the White House. You can see why they are called the Red Room, Green Room, and Blue Room.

The Diplomatic Reception Room and the State Dining Room are used for these events. There can be as many as 140 guests for dinner! Afterward, music, singing, or dancing often takes place in the East Room.

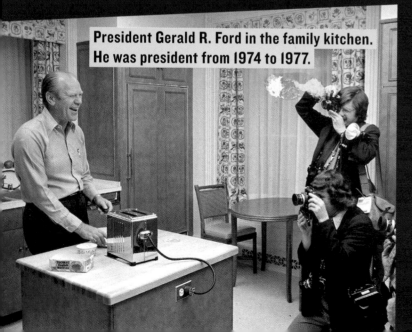

The Obama family watches the 2011 World Cup soccer game at home in the White House.

President Gerald R. Ford in the family kitchen. He was president from 1974 to 1977.

The president and first lady can leave work and go upstairs to their private floor. Each first family can decorate this second-floor space, but they can't change much in the rest of the White House.

President Richard M. Nixon and his family in their White House living room. He was president from 1969 to 1974.

Upstairs at the White House, the first family can cook in their own kitchen. They can hang out in their own living room. Children of presidents can invite friends up for sleepovers. It's a home within a house—but of course, there are Secret Service agents guarding the entrance!

First Lady Nancy Reagan reads mail in the same room.

First Lady Michelle Obama jumps double-dutch in front of the White House.

The first family and their guests can relax outside in the White House pool, shoot hoops on the basketball court, or run around the jogging track.

President William J. Clinton jogs on the White House track. He served from 1993 to 2001.

President Lyndon B. Johnson in the White House pool with his grandson and dog. LBJ was president from 1963 to 1969.

Inside the White House, there is a bowling alley and a theater for watching movies or TV.

The White House is also an important museum. It contains books, china, furniture, art, and other objects that have been given to the presidents or bought for the White House.

Abraham Lincoln, who served from 1861 to 1865, never slept in this bed in the room named after him. But guests of the president do! This photo is from 1992. Like other rooms in the White House, it has been changed over time.

First Lady Laura Bush in the White House Library

The contents of the White House trace the history of the United States. It is the White House curator's job to research and take care of all these things.

On February 14, 1962, First Lady Jacqueline Kennedy (right) gave the first televised tour of the White House. She played an important part in restoring the White House and getting many of the objects that are in it. Her husband, John F. Kennedy, was president from 1961 to 1963.

Washing the White House windows

Painting the White House, 1921

Getting flowers ready to use in the White House

It takes many, many people to keep a house with 132 rooms clean and working smoothly. Household staff care for the public rooms. Chefs and waiters cook, serve, and clear meals. Gardeners take care of the 18 acres of lawns and gardens surrounding the White House.

First Lady Michelle Obama created a vegetable garden at the White House.

That includes the President's Park, which has a vegetable garden, famous old trees, and an even more famous rose garden. There is also a children's garden with handprints and footprints of presidential children and grandchildren. And let's not forget painters! It takes 570 gallons of paint to make sure the White House lives up to its name.

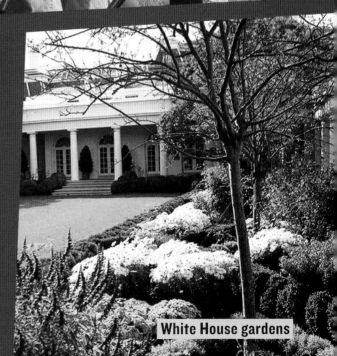

White House gardens

How would you like to be a first child and call the
White House home? Wouldn't it be fun to live in a place with
132 rooms,
35 bathrooms,
147 windows,
412 doors,
28 fireplaces,

8 staircases,
3 elevators,
more than 2,700 books in the library,
a pool, a bowling alley,
a movie theater . . .

and all that history?

GLOSSARY

architect: a person who designs buildings

capital: the city in a country or state where the government is based

Congress: the branch of the US government that makes laws

curator: the person in charge of a museum or art collection

portico: a porch or walkway with a roof that is supported by columns

press: people whose job it is to record and report news

restoring: bringing something back to the way it was, or cleaning and fixing it

swamp: an area of wet, spongy ground, a marsh

televised: shown on television